Pomeranian

Pom Pom Ado

by Sunita Apte

Consultant: Connie Zieba, Pomeranian Exhibitor
Corresponding Secretary, Pomeranian Club of Greater Houston

BEARPORT
PUBLISHING

New York, New York

Credits

Cover and Title Page, © Suponev Vladmir Mihajlovich; TOC, © Suponev Vladmir Mihajlovich/Shutterstock; 4, Courtesy of Kathy Fornataro; 5, Courtesy of Kathy Fornataro; 6, Courtesy of Gary Cooper/Bridgeton News; 7, Courtesy of Kathy Fornataro; 8, © Close Encounters of the Furry Kind/kimballstock; 9, © tbkmedia.de/Alamy; 10, © Tate, London/Art Resource, NY; 11, The Royal Collection © 2008, Her Majesty Queen Elizabeth II; 12, © Carlo Allegri/Getty Images; 13, © Gene Blevins/Corbis; 14, © Pets by Paulette; 15L, © Jerry Shulman/SuperStock; 15R, © Cheryl Ertelt/Visuals Unlimited; 16, © Dwight Dyke; 17, © AFP Photo/Johnny Green/Newscom; 18, © James O'Connor; 19, © Bonnie Nance/Rural Images; 20, © Pets by Paulette; 21, © Yoshio Tomii/SuperStock; 22, © Connie Zieba; 23, © Sam Panthaky/AFP/Getty Images; 24, © Cheri Fults; 25, © Frank Siteman/Photo Edit; 26, © William Hillman; 27, © Courtesy Canon USA; 28, © N Joy Neish/Shutterstock; 29, © Tracy Morgan/Dorling Kindersley; 31, © Michelle D. Milliman/Shutterstock; 32, © Suponev Vladmir Mihajlovich/Shutterstock

Publisher: Kenn Goin
Senior Editor: Lisa Wiseman
Creative Director: Spencer Brinker
Photo Researcher: Amy Dunleavy
Design: Dawn Beard Creative

Library of Congress Cataloging-in-Publication Data

Apte, Sunita.
  Pomeranian : pom pom ado / by Sunita Apte.
    p. cm. — (Little dogs rock!)
  Includes bibliographical references.
  ISBN-13: 978-1-59716-745-1 (library binding)
  ISBN-10: 1-59716-745-2 (library binding)
  1. Pomeranian dog—Juvenile literature. I. Title.

  SF429.P8A64 2009
  636.76—dc22
                    2008033892

For more information, write to Bearport Publishing Company, Inc., 101 Fifth Avenue, Suite 6R, New York, New York 10003. Printed in the United States of America in North Mankato, Minnesota.

122009
111709CG

10 9 8 7 6 5 4 3 2

Contents

Little Lifesaver

Kathy Fornataro sat sadly in her home in Rosenhayn, New Jersey. She had recently learned that her tiny, beloved Pomeranian (pom-*uh*-RAYN-ee-un), Ginger, was very sick. Ginger was old and her heart was failing. Kathy couldn't stand the thought of losing her.

▲ **Ginger at home**

Suddenly, Kathy's front door burst open. An **intruder** had forced his way into her home. Kathy froze, terrified. The man told Kathy that he had harmed her husband. Would he do the same to her?

Kathy didn't have a chance to find out. Without warning, Ginger lunged at the intruder, biting him on the ankle.

▲ **Ginger has fun with a family friend.**

Pomeranians, nicknamed Poms, usually weigh from three to seven pounds (1.4 to 3.2 kg). Their small size makes these tiny dogs popular pets.

Toothless Wonder

Ginger's bite couldn't have hurt too badly. She was old and nearly toothless. Still, it startled the man so much that he kicked Ginger across the room. The five-pound (2.3-kg) dog flew through the air like a soccer ball.

Kathy, terrified that her dog was hurt, rushed over to Ginger. She cradled the Pomeranian in her arms. Then as quickly as he had entered the house, the intruder swiftly turned around and fled.

Ginger and Kathy

Four police officers caught and arrested the man a short time later. It turned out that he hadn't harmed Kathy's husband at all. Luckily for Kathy, little Ginger had managed to scare away a **criminal** and save her life.

Pomeranians are not considered dangerous animals. However, they will always try to protect their owners.

For her heroic work, Ginger was inducted into the New Jersey Animal Hall of Fame.

Sled Dogs to Small Dogs

Pomeranians are a tiny, or **toy**, dog **breed**. However, they weren't always so small. Pomeranians are **descendants** of an ancient sled dog known as the Spitz. Hundreds of years ago, Spitz dogs lived in cold, snowy areas where people traveled by sled. These dogs were big and strong so that they could pull heavy loads.

▲ **American Eskimo dogs are related to Pomeranians. Both breeds are descendants of ancient Spitz dogs.**

By the 1500s, Spitz dogs were popular in an area of Europe known as Pomerania. There, the dogs were bred to be smaller. These new, littler dogs were named Pomeranians, after the area.

The first Poms were much bigger than today's tiny dogs, however. They often weighed as much as 30 pounds (13.6 kg).

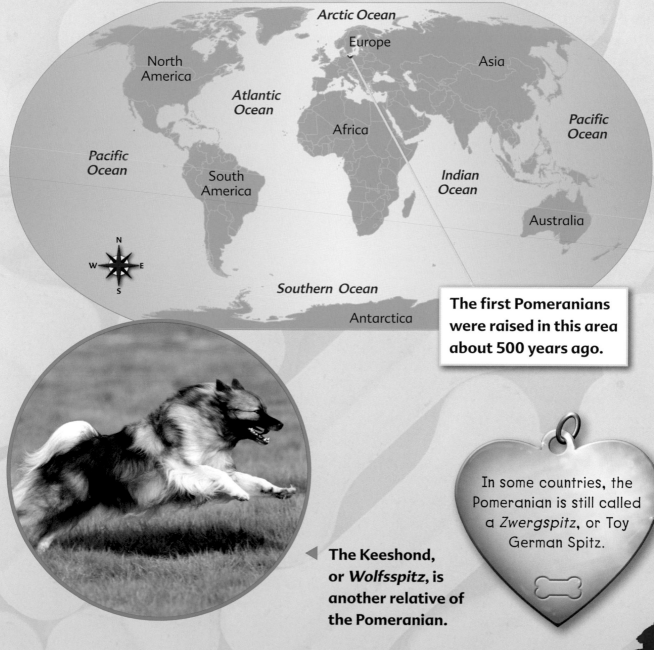

The first Pomeranians were raised in this area about 500 years ago.

◀ The Keeshond, or *Wolfsspitz*, is another relative of the Pomeranian.

In some countries, the Pomeranian is still called a *Zwergspitz*, or Toy German Spitz.

Royal Pets

In the 1700s, Queen Charlotte of England brought the first Pomeranians from Pomerania to her country. These beautiful animals became very popular with English **royalty**. However, they were still large, weighing 20 pounds (9 kg) or more.

▲ **Queen Charlotte's Pomeranians, shown here, were white and much larger than Poms today.**

Then, in 1888, Queen Charlotte's granddaughter, Queen Victoria, brought a 12-pound (5.4-kg) Pom named Marco back from Italy. She fell in love with this little dog and began breeding Pomeranians, making them smaller and smaller. Eventually, they reached the toy size that they are today.

Soon these new, tiny Pomeranians crossed the Atlantic Ocean and became popular in the United States. In 1900, the **American Kennel Club** (AKC) recognized the Pomeranian as an official breed.

Some historians say that at one time Queen Victoria had 35 pet Poms.

▲ **This painting, called "Marco on the Breakfast Table," shows the beloved pet that Queen Victoria brought back from Italy.**

The Popular Pom

Pomeranians got their start as royal pets, and today they're still popular with the rich and famous. Many celebrities have pet Poms. For example, singer Britney Spears owns a Pomeranian named Izzy. Basketball player Kobe Bryant has one named Gucci. Movie star Hilary Duff is the proud owner of three—Macy, Bentley, and Griffin.

◀ **Hilary Duff (left) and her sister, Haylie (right), with one of their pet Poms**

The Italian painter Michelangelo had a pet Pom. Some historians say that the small dog sat next to Michelangelo while he painted the ceiling of the Sistine Chapel in the 1500s.

Since the dogs are so small, stars often carry their Poms around with them. TV star Nicole Richie is famous for taking her Pomeranian, Foxxy Cleopatra, almost everywhere with her.

People that aren't famous love Poms, too. For at least the past ten years, Poms have ranked in the top 15 in the AKC list of most popular dog breeds.

▲ **Nicole Richie's dog, Foxxy Cleopatra, is becoming almost as well known as her celebrity owner.**

Pom Colors Aplenty

Unlike most dogs, Pomeranians have two **coats** of fur. The undercoat is thick, soft, and fluffy. The overcoat on top, is long, straight, and **coarse**. These two coats can be the same color or different colors.

The original Poms that Queen Charlotte brought to England were white, while Queen Victoria's Marco was reddish-brown. Today, Pomeranians come in all sorts of colors. They can be solid red, orange, black, brown, cream, sable, white, and blue, which looks gray.

A brindle Pom, a cream-colored Pom, and a red Pom

Many Poms have multicolored coats or patterns. For example, a parti-colored Pom has more than one color in its overcoat. A brindle Pom has light stripes on its fur.

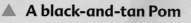

Most parti-colored Poms have white coats with patches of another color on them.

▲ **A black-and-tan Pom**

Orange is the most common coat color for Pomeranians.

Small Size, Large Responsibility

For many pet owners, a Pom's small size has advantages. They're the perfect pets for apartments or small houses. They don't require as much food or exercise as bigger dogs. They're also easy to carry around and can go with their owners almost anywhere.

However, their small size also makes these animals **vulnerable**. Pomeranians can hurt themselves jumping off of furniture. If they don't watch where they're walking, they can be stepped on and seriously injured.

Despite their heavy coats, sometimes Poms need a little extra protection in the cold weather.

Like most small dogs, Pomeranians can live for a long time. It's not unusual for one to live 15 years or more.

Pet owners need to keep a sharp eye on their Poms. The animals should never be left alone outdoors, except in a safe, fenced-in yard. Otherwise, they risk being attacked by bigger dogs or other animals, such as coyotes.

▲ **Poms are not afraid of bigger dogs because they actually seem to think they're big themselves.**

Pom Pom Problems

To stay healthy and look their best, Poms require special care. Their nails need to be trimmed often, and their long coats need regular **grooming**. They should be brushed carefully several times a week.

Foxy's owner brushes her coat.

Most Poms **shed** their undercoats about once a year. Shedding can be frustrating for owners, whose clothes and furniture become covered with dog fur.

Pomeranians are prone to losing their teeth because their teeth are so small. So owners need to make sure their dogs have good dental care. They should take their pets to the **veterinarian** yearly to have their teeth examined. They also must brush their dogs' teeth at least once a week.

Small dogs like Pomeranians also gain weight easily. Owners have to be careful not to overfeed their dogs or give them too many treats. Overweight Poms can develop serious health problems, such as **diabetes**.

▲ **A Pom getting its teeth brushed**

Pomeranian Puppies

Pomeranian puppies are very small. They can weigh as little as one ounce (28 g) at birth, though healthier puppies usually weigh three ounces (85 g) or more.

Pomeranian **litters** are also small. On average only one to three puppies are born at the same time, compared to six or more in larger breeds.

▲ **A Pom pup at six weeks old**

Pom puppies begin to shed their coats starting at about three months of age. Their adult coats don't fully grow in until they're two years old.

After Pom pups are born, they need to stay with their mothers, brothers, and sisters until they're at least two months old. In fact, some breeders keep Pom puppies with their mothers until they're three to six months old. During this time, the little ones learn how to eat, take care of themselves, and be around other dogs and people.

A puppy's coat color can change a lot as it grows. Generally, the best way to figure out what color a Pom will be is to look at its parents and grandparents.

Training a Pom

Pomeranians are smart dogs that are usually easy to train. However, because of their small size, Poms have small **bladders**, and can be harder to **housetrain** than other dogs. Often, though, they can be taught to use a litter box just like a cat.

Pomeranians make good guard dogs because they naturally bark when a stranger is near. In some cases, too much barking can be a problem, especially for Poms that live in apartments. They must be trained not to make a lot of noise.

Keoki is a well-trained Pom. Here, he is jumping over an obstacle during a dog show.

Sometimes Poms feel **threatened** by small children and need time to adjust to living with them. They do, however, get along very well with adults and other animals in their households. Their lively, energetic nature makes them really fun to be around!

Like wolves, dogs like to be part of a group, or **pack**. A well-trained dog views its owner as the pack leader.

Big Helper

Don't let their small size fool you. Even though they're small, Poms make great working dogs. For example, some Poms work as **search and rescue dogs**, finding people trapped after accidents or disasters. Poms are good at this job because they're easy to train and small enough to fit in tight spaces.

Poms are also great **therapy dogs**. Their small size and sweet nature make them good pets—and friends—for people who are feeling lonely or sad.

▲ Sophie, a therapy dog, visits with Rose Courtney. Rose says that "holding Sophie reminds her of holding her own children when they were babies."

Some Poms, such a Mica, are trained as **hearing dogs** because they're smart and willing to please. These dogs alert their human owners who are **deaf**, or have trouble hearing, to important sounds, such as a phone ringing or a knock on the door. Mica will nuzzle her owner's hand and go over to the door when she hears a knock.

▲ **Mica was rescued from a shelter and trained as a hearing dog. Here, she wakes up her owner after hearing the alarm clock go off.**

Some hearing dogs even help their deaf or **hearing-impaired** owners read lips. The dog looks at the person who is speaking. Then the owner looks in the same direction as the dog, so he or she always knows who is talking.

Poms in the Spotlight

Poms are not only the pets of celebrities, they're also famous themselves. They have had their share of roles on both the big and small screens. For example, Poms have been featured in such hit movies as *Superman Returns* (2006) and *Titanic* (1997).

A Pomeranian even landed the title role in the movie *Quigley* (2003). In the film, a dog-hating **billionaire** is turned into a white Pom named Quigley. Throughout the movie, Quigley does many clever and funny things, including using a computer.

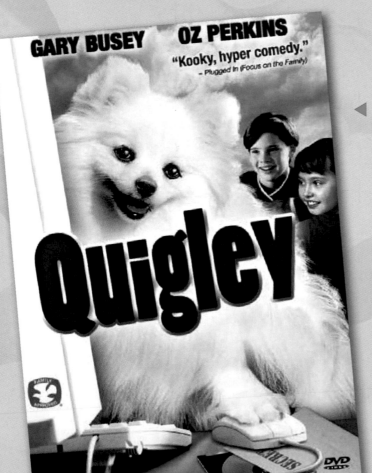

 Quigley was actually played by three Pomeranians—Willow, Sasha, and Maui.

When the famous ship the *Titanic* hit an iceberg and sank in 1912, two of the three dogs rescued in lifeboats were Pomeranians.

Another Pom actor named Beowolf has appeared on TV. He stars as tennis champion Maria Sharapova's dog in a series of Canon camera commercials.

Poms are popular on-screen for the same reasons they're popular in real life. These beautiful and charming dogs are beloved by all who encounter them.

▲ Tennis champion Maria Sharapova has her own Pomeranian, named Dolce. However, Beowolf, a dog that has been trained to act, was brought in to work with her in the Canon commercials.

Pomeranians at a Glance

Weight:	Usually 3 to 7 pounds (1.4 to 3.2 kg); can sometimes weigh up to 12 pounds (5.4 kg)
Height:	8 to 11 inches (20 to 28 cm)
Colors:	Many solid colors, including red, orange, cream, sable, black, brown, blue, and white; various patterns, including brindle, parti-colored, and tricolored tan
Area of Origin:	Pomerania (today's Germany and Poland)
Life Span:	About 15 years
Personality:	Sociable, smart, loyal, and lively; not afraid of strangers or bigger dogs

Best in Show

What makes a great Pomeranian? Every owner knows that his or her dog is special. Judges in dog shows, however, look very carefully at a Pomeranian's appearance and behavior. Here are some of the things they look for:

tiny ears sit high on the head

head should be in balance with the body, with an alert, fox-like face

eyes are dark, medium-size, and almond-shaped

big fluffy tail lies flat and straight on the back

Behavior: should be energetic, smart, and outgoing

feet are tiny and arched

soft, thick undercoat and a long, straight, coarse overcoat

body and legs should be in proportion, which means that neither should be much shorter or longer than the other

Glossary

American Kennel Club
(uh-MER-uh-kuhn KEN-uhl KLUHB)
a national organization that is involved in many activities having to do with dogs, including collecting information about dog breeds and setting rules for dog shows

billionaire (BIL-yuhn-*air*) a person whose wealth is a billion dollars or more

bladders (BLAD-urz) organs found in people or animals that store liquid wastes before they leave the body.

breed (BREED) a group of dogs that look very much alike

coarse (KORSS) a rough texture

coats (KOHTS) the fur on dogs or other animals

criminal (KRIH-min-uhl) a person who breaks the law

deaf (DEF) not able to hear

descendants (di-SEND-uhnts) living things that are related to other living things from the past

diabetes (*dye*-uh-BEE-teez) a disease in which a person or animal's blood has too much sugar in it; if not treated, it can lead to blindness or heart disease

grooming (GROOM-ing) combing and washing an animal's coat

hearing dogs (HEER-ing DAWGZ) dogs that help their hearing-impaired owners live independently

hearing-impaired (HIHR-ing-im-PAIRD) not being able to hear very well

housetrain (HAUS-trayn) to teach an animal to go to the bathroom outside

intruder (in-TROOD-ur) someone who enters a place forcefully

litters (LIT-urz) groups of animals that are born to the same mother at the same time

pack (PAK) a group of animals that live and travel together under one leader

royalty (ROY-uhl-tee) kings, queens, princesses, and princes

search and rescue dogs (SURCH AND RES-kyoo DAWGZ) dogs that look for survivors after a disaster, such as an earthquake

shed (SHED) to lose hair or fur

therapy dogs (THER-uh-pee DAWGZ) dogs that visit places such as hospitals to cheer up people and make them feel more comfortable

threatened (THRET-uhnd) being in immediate danger

toy (TOY) tiny, when relating to dogs

veterinarian (*vet*-ur-uh-NER-ee-uhn) a doctor who takes care of dogs and other animals

vulnerable (VUHL-nuhr-uh-bull) able to be easily hurt

Bibliography

Coile, D. Caroline. *Pomeranians for Dummies.* Hoboken, NJ: Wiley Publishing Inc. (2007).

Grant, Lexiann. *The Pomeranian.* Neptune City, NJ: TFH Publications (2006).

Moreno, Julie. *A New Owner's Guide to Pomeranians.* Neptune City, NJ: TFH Publications (2000).

Vanderlip, Sharon L. *The Pomeranian Handbook.* Hauppauge, NY: Barron's (2007).

Read More

The American Kennel Club. *The Complete Dog Book for Kids.* Hoboken, NJ: John Wiley (1996).

Fiege, Sharon N. *Littlebit Goes a Long Way.* Bloomington, IN: AuthorHouse (2007).

Mehus-Roe, Kristin. *Dogs for Kids!: Everything You Need to Know About Dogs.* Irvine, CA: BowTie Press (2007).

Learn More Online

To learn more about Pomeranians, visit
www.bearportpublishing.com/LittleDogsRock

Index

About the Author

Sunita Apte has written more than forty books for children and teens.
A dog lover, Sunita resides in Brooklyn, New York.